NOPQRSTUVWXYZ
nopqrstuvwxyz
NOPQRSTUVWXYZ
nopqrstuvwxyz
NOPQRSTUVWXYZ
nopqrstuvwxyz
NOPQRSTUVWXYZ
nopqrstuvwxyz

DK

www.dk.com

Project Editor Monica Byles
Art Editor Jane Horne
Production Jayne Wood
Photography Steve Gorton, Tim Ridley,
and Andy Crawford

Published in Great Britain by
Dorling Kindersley Limited,
9 Henrietta Street, London WC2E 8PS

4 6 8 10 9 7 5

First published by Dorling Kindersley in 1993, reprinted 1994, 1995 and 1999.

Text and photographs copyright © 1993, 1999 Dorling Kindersley Limited, London

Photography (lion) copyright © 1990 Jerry Young; (weevil, yellow back stag beetle,
jewel beetle, red-spotted longhorn beetle, lion, monkey) copyright © 1991 Jerry Young

Illustrations Chris Fisher
Wooden alphabet Simon Money and Paul Scannell

Additional Photography Paul Bricknell, Jane Burton, Peter Chadwick, Gordon Clayton,
Geoff Dann, Philip Dowell, Mike Dunning, Andreas von Einsiedel, Jo Foord,
Frank Greenaway, Stephen Hayward, David Johnson, Colin Keates, Dave King,
Cyril Laubscher, Graham Miller, David Murray, Stephen Oliver, Daniel Pangbourne,
Roger Phillips, Karl Shone, Steve Shott, Kim Taylor, Jerry Young.

Dorling Kindersley would also like to thank Gregory Coleman, Lauren Doona,
Junji Hoshika, Tonya Kamil, Corinne Laidlaw, Gemma Loke, Perry Medland,
Daisy Mooney, Nicholas Papsworth, Sarah Pearce, Anthony Singh, Milo Taylor,
and Christina Wilson for appearing in this book.

A CIP catalogue record for this book is available from the British Library.

ISBN 0-7513-5071-0

Colour reproduction
Printed and boun

Note to parents

My First ABC is designed to
stimulate children's curiosity about
the letters of the alphabet. Each page is
packed with bright, colourful pictures of
familiar things to capture children's attention
and to encourage them to talk about their
own interests and experiences.

As you read the book together, try to give
each letter as much personal meaning as you can.
Young children's first awareness of letters is usually
centred around their own names, and the names
of other people, or experiences that are
important to them. Making these sorts of
personal connections makes it easier for your
child to remember what individual letters
look like, and what they are called.

Make learning about the letters fun
by playing games with them. Play
hunt-the-letter together when
looking at the words on each page,
and listen for the sounds that
individual letters make when
you say the words. Show your child how to sing
along the alphabet at the bottom of the page, pointing
with your finger to each capital letter as you go. Encourage
your child to follow the progress of Alphie the Alphabet
Builder and predict which letter he will introduce on the
next page. Trace the shape of each letter with a finger
and talk about how it is formed. This will help your
child to write it.

Above all, use your child's interest as a guide. Because
My First ABC is full of vivid and interesting pictures, you
will find that children want to return to it frequently to read
and re-read it. Each time they will learn a little more about
the letters and about the alphabet, and
gain a stronger view of themselves
as "readers".

Jane Bunting
Author

ABCDEFGHIJKLMN

8.99

MY FIRST
abc

Jane Bunting

DK

LONDON • NEW YORK • SYDNEY • MOSCOW

OPQRSTUVWXYZ

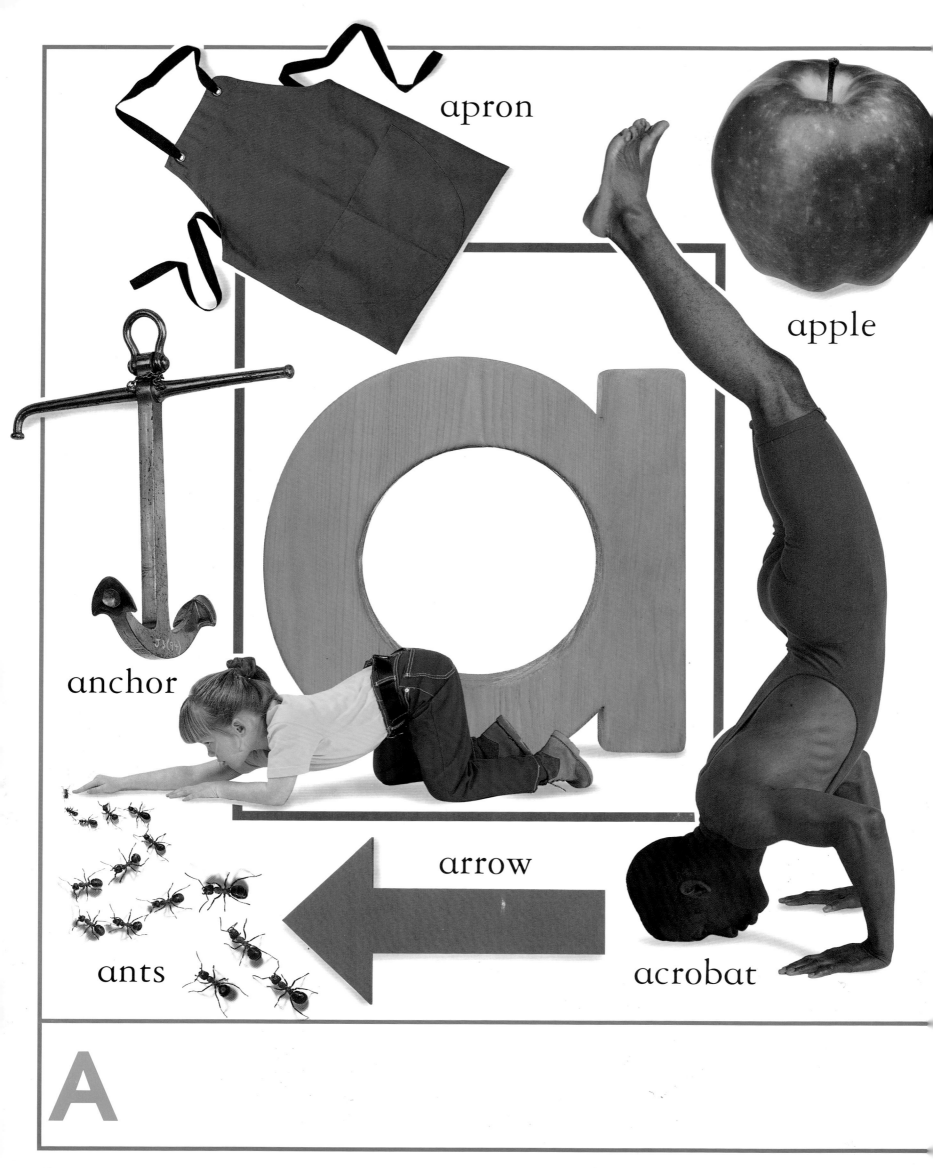

apron

apple

anchor

anchor

arrow

ants

acrobat

A

6

butterfly

book

balloons

baby

bowl

blue

bear

beads

ball

boat

B

cap

crayon

cat

clock

candles

car

chair

combs

crocodile

AB C

drum

dolphin

doll

door

dinosaur

duck

ducklings

daisy

dog

elephant

envelope

egg

fish

fan

flower

feather

fruit

fork

ABCD **E** F

10

glasses

giraffe

goldfish

game

guitar

gorilla

green

glove

goose

11

honey

helicopter

hammer

hat

hairbrush

horn

horse

ABCDEFG H

12

ice cream

insects

ink

iguana

jigsaw
puzzle

jeans

jacket

juice

jewellery

jack-in-the-box

ABCDEFGHI J

kitten

kite

key

king

kiwi

knot

kangaroo

15

leaves

lizard

lamb

lemon

lamp

ladder

lion

lettuce

ABCDEFGHIJK **L**

16

money

marbles

mirror

milk

m

mask

monkey

melon

magnet

M

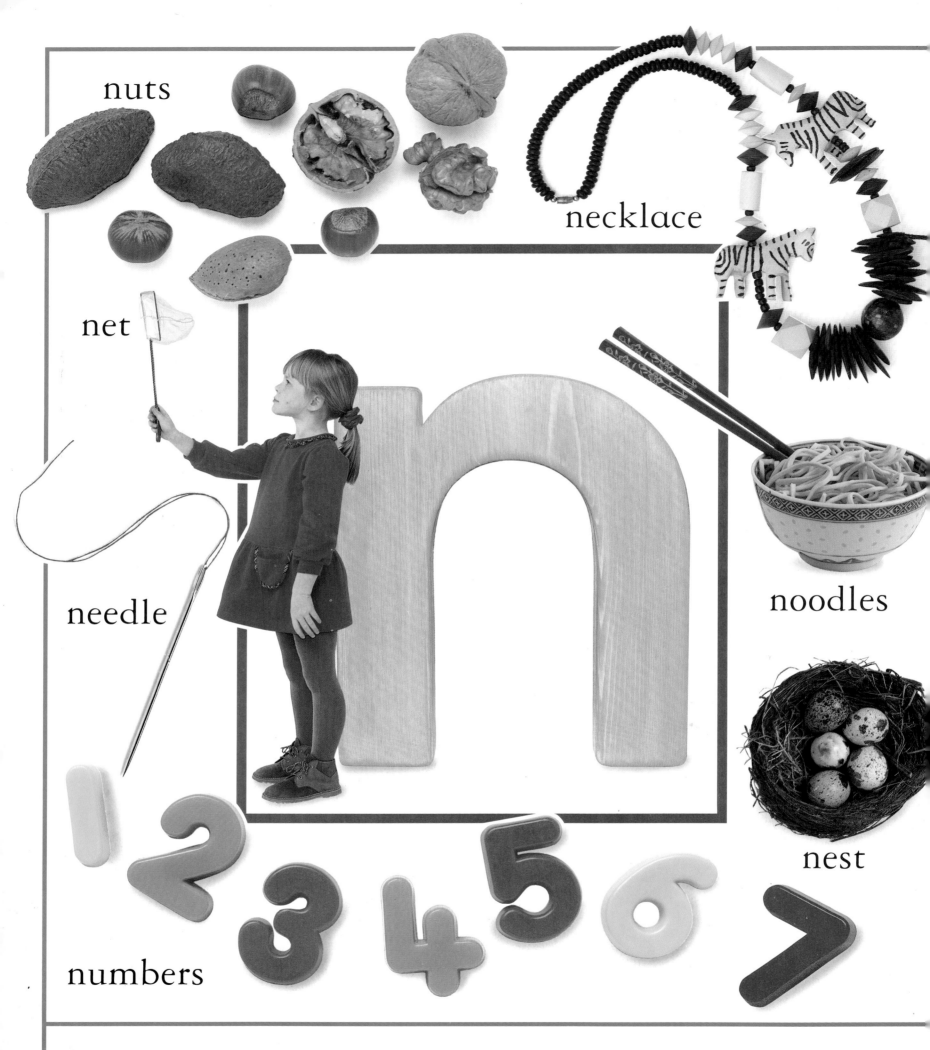

nuts

necklace

net

noodles

needle

nest

1 2 3 4 5 6 7

numbers

ABCDEFGHIJKLMN

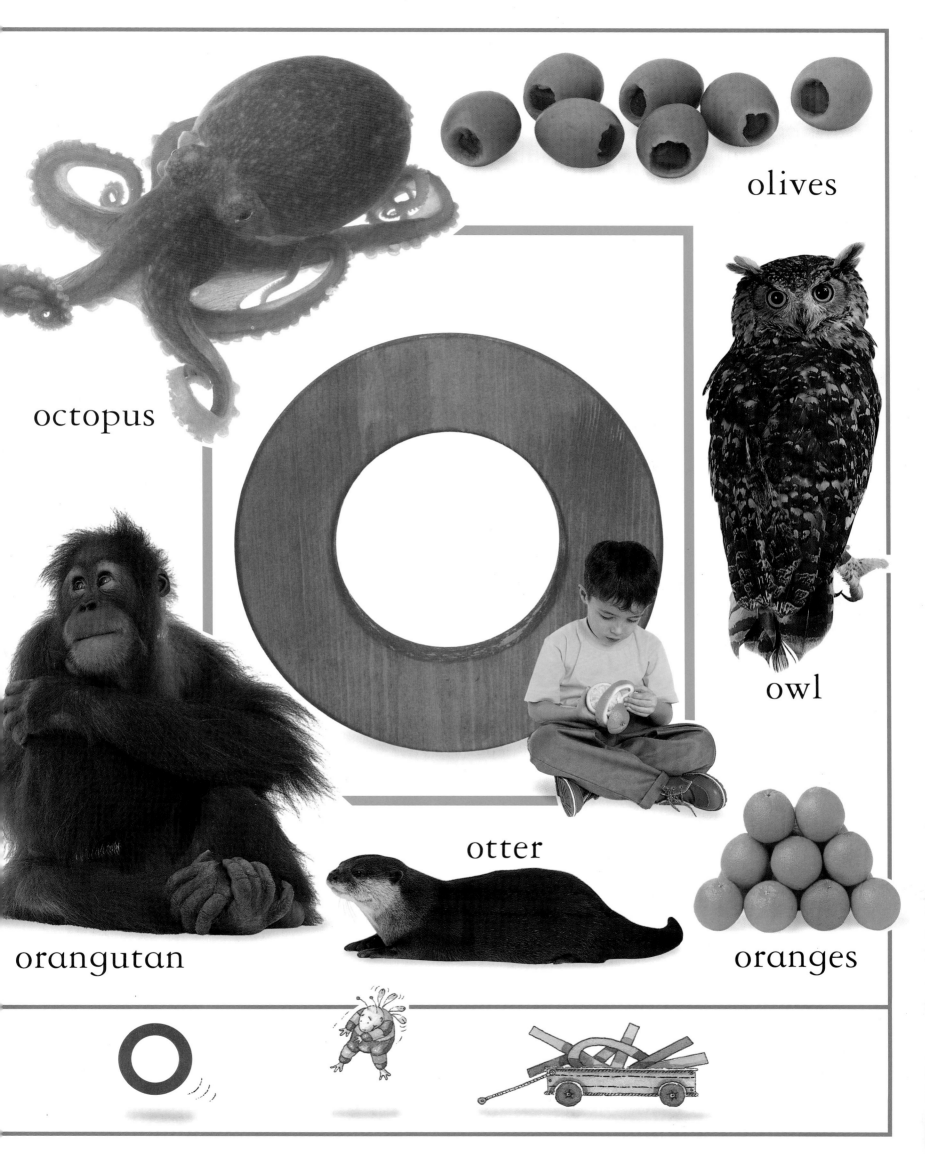

olives

octopus

owl

orangutan

otter

oranges

pineapple

penguin

puppy

pencil

puppet

queen

present

paint

ABCDEFGHIJ KLMN

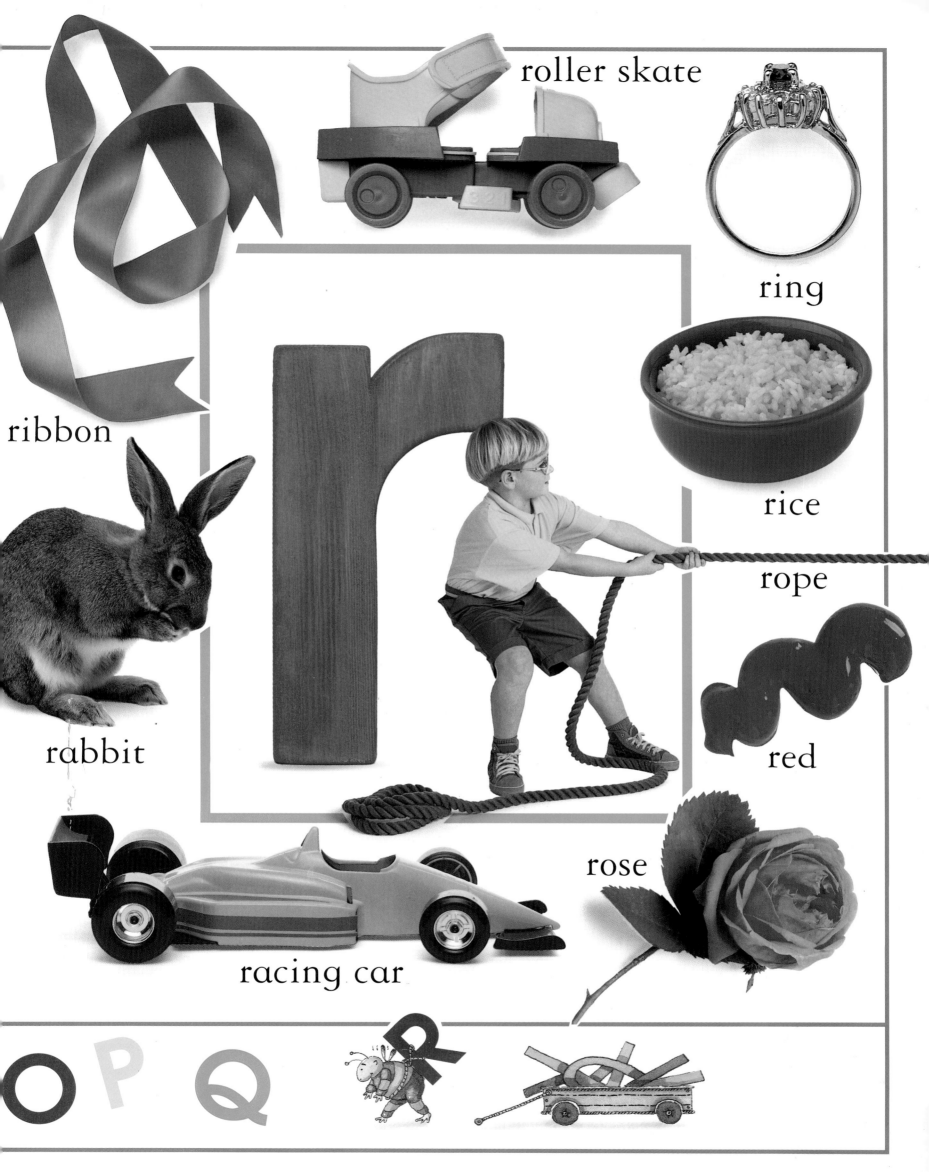

roller skate

ring

ribbon

rice

rope

rabbit

red

rose

racing car

r

O P Q R

21

squirrel

snake

socks

seahorse

sand

shells

spoon

scarf

ABCDEFGHIJKLMN

22

toothbrush

tractor

teddy bear

t

tiger

tomato

telephone

train

O P Q R S

underwear

violin

umbrella

vulture

vase

vegetables

U V

ABCDEFGHIJKLMN

24

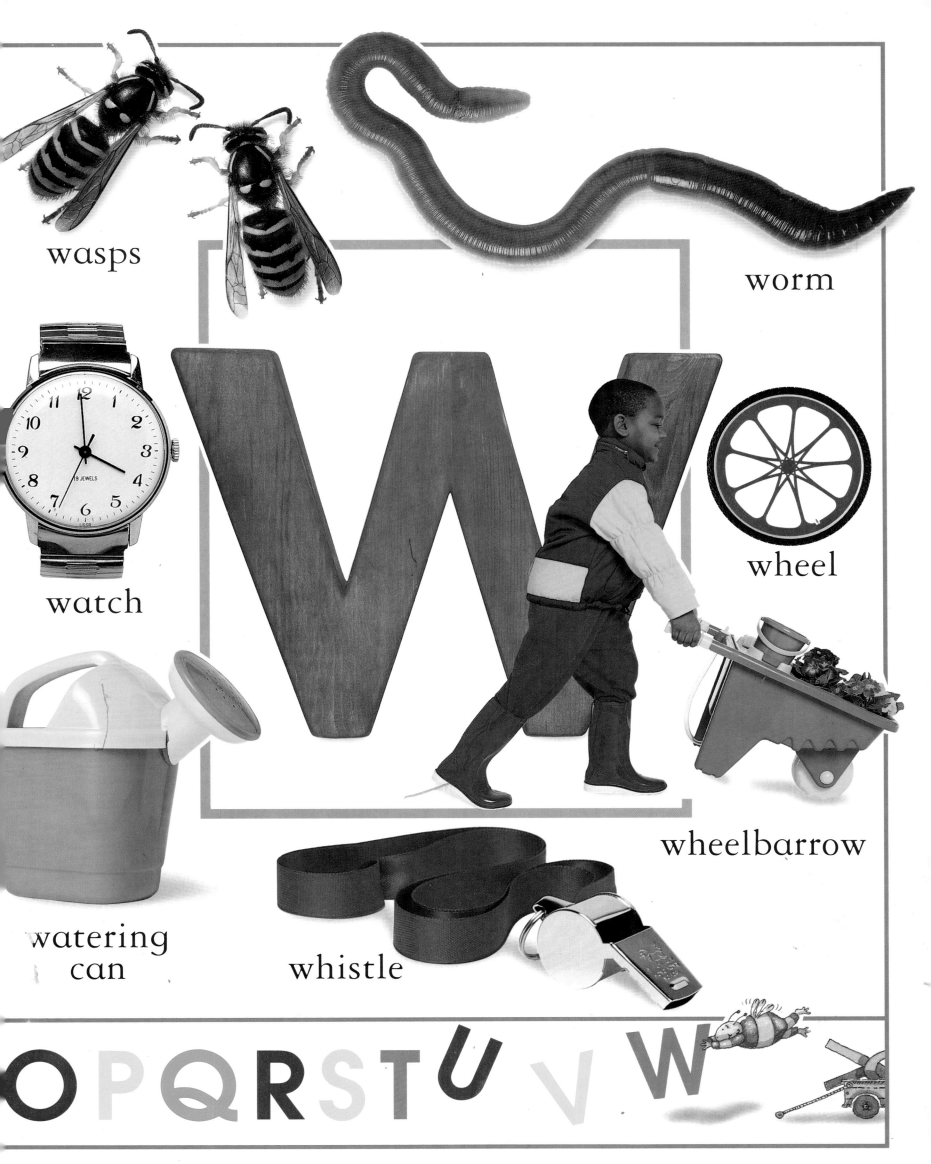

wasps

worm

watch

wheel

watering
can

whistle

wheelbarrow

xylophone

yo-yo

yellow

yoghurt

yolk

yam

zebra

zero

zip

zigzag

O P Q R S T U V W X Y Z

27

ABC games

- Can you match up each word with its picture?

- Use the pictures to play "I spy" with a friend. Take it in turns to choose a picture and say which letter it begins with. Can your friend guess which picture you have chosen?

- Make your name with pictures. Take each letter in turn and find the object that begins with that letter.

ABCDEFGHIJ KLMN